PIONEERS OF SCIENCE

JOSEPH LISTER

Douglas McTavish

Pioneers of Science

05223394

Archimedes
Alexander Graham Bell
Karl Benz
Marie Curie
Thomas Edison
Albert Einstein
Michael Faraday
Alexander Fleming
Galileo
Edward Jenner
Joseph Lister
Guglielmo Marconi
Isaac Newton
Louis Pasteur
Leonardo da Vinci
James Watt

Series and book editor Rosemary Ashley
Designer David Armitage

First published in 1991 by
Wayland (Publishers) Ltd
61 Western Road, Hove
East Sussex BN3 1JD, England

British Library Cataloguing in Publication Data
McTavish, Douglas
    Joseph Lister. – (Pioneers of science)
    I. Title   II. Series
    617.092

    ISBN 0 7502 0168 1

Typeset by DP Press Ltd, Sevenoaks, Kent
Printed in Italy by Rotolito Lombarda S.p.A.
Bound in France by A.G.M.

Contents

1 ▽ Early Life

Joseph Lister was born on 5 April 1827 at Upton House in West Ham, just outside London. Upton House was an impressive mansion with a large garden, set in open countryside. His family were originally from Bingley, a small town on the Yorkshire moors, and Joseph's great-grandfather had moved to London to work as a tobacconist in 1720. Both Joseph's grandfather and father were wine merchants in London, and his father, in particular, was very successful.

Joseph Lister senior was, however, more than just a wealthy wine merchant. His hobby was observing things through a microscope and recording what he saw. He also invented a special lens for his microscope which enabled him to see minute objects even more clearly. His new lens was what is known as 'achromatic'; that is, it was

London in about 1830. Joseph Lister was born outside the city, at West Ham, in 1827.

Lister's father, also called Joseph, was keenly interested in observing things through a microscope. He even invented a special lens that enabled him to see small objects more clearly.

of a shape that reduced the problems caused by light splitting into its 'rainbow' colours when passing through a lens. This invention won him election to the most important scientific institution in the country – the Royal Society.

Young Joseph's family were Quakers – members of the Society of Friends, a Christian sect founded in about 1650. Quakers believe that worship should be carried out in a quiet, simple way without the elaborate rituals performed by other Christian Churches. When he was eight years old, Joseph went to a Quaker school in Hertfordshire, and later attended the Grove School in Tottenham, North London.

This page from Lister's sketchbook contains wildlife drawings that he made when he was a young boy.

As a child Joseph was very interested in nature study, and the garden and surrounding countryside at Upton House gave him plenty of opportunities to observe and draw plants and animals. By the time he left school in 1844, he had already decided that he wanted to be a doctor. He enrolled as a student at University College in London where, after three years, he gained a Bachelor of Arts degree. This meant that he could go on to become a medical student, and in 1848 he prepared himself for two more years of study at the University College Hospital.

Nowadays we often take medical science for granted. We know that if we become ill our doctors will almost certainly be able to discover what is wrong and treat us. Even if we need to go into hospital for an operation, there is an extremely high probability that the treatment will be effective.

Things were very different at the time when Lister was studying medicine. Many of the illnesses that we now know how to treat had not even been identified, and people frequently died from diseases that modern medicine has almost wiped out – such as polio, tuberculosis and diphtheria. Being ill was bad enough, but having to undergo an operation was very much worse.

The squalor and dirt of London and other large cities in the nineteenth century provided a breeding ground for infectious diseases. Even simple wounds could easily become infected, often leading to death.

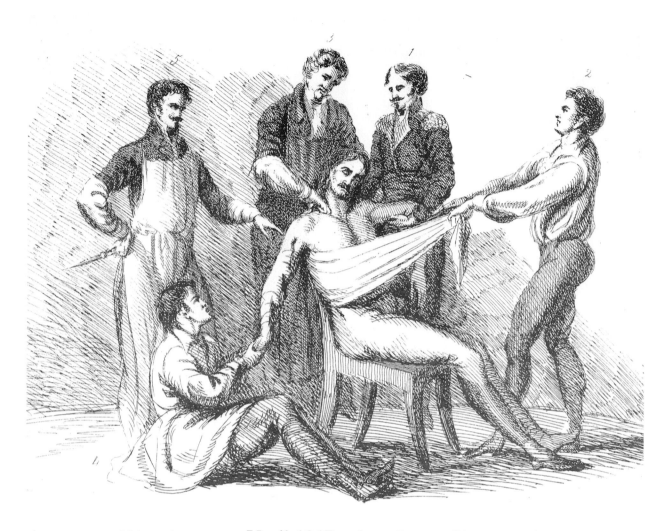

A surgeon and his assistants prepare to amputate a man's arm at the shoulder. This picture first appeared in 1821 in a book entitled Illustrations of the Great Operations of Surgery *by Charles Bell. The author commented that the amputation had to be done rapidly, and that the knife should be used 'more like a sabre than surgeon's scalpel'.*

Until 1847, when James Simpson discovered the value of chloroform, there were no truly effective anaesthetics. Not only was surgery frequently horribly painful; it also put the patients' lives in great danger. The chances of surviving even minor surgery were not high and after a major operation, such as amputation (cutting off) of a limb, they were less than 50 per cent. Although surgeons did their best, and many were doubtless very skilful, as soon as the patient's skin was cut there was the risk that the flesh would decay and the blood become poisoned. This was known as sepsis. There was nothing doctors could do once sepsis set in, and the patient's survival then became purely a matter of luck.

A surgical operation before Lister

Until Lister's time, operations were both extremely painful and highly dangerous. This illustration, dating from the eighteenth century, shows a man having his right leg amputated above the knee. He would not have been given any anaesthetic except, perhaps, a large quantity of alcohol to lessen the pain. The surgeon needed three assistants just to keep his patient still. Even when James Simpson discovered the value of chloroform as an anaesthetic, in 1847, many of his fellow surgeons resisted using it for some years.

The other tragic aspect of this operation is the fact that having endured so much pain the patient stood only a slim chance of survival, simply because no one knew why it was that infections occurred after surgery. The surgeon, his assistants and the patient are all shown dressed in their normal clothes, which would have carried dust and germs, and the saw being used for the amputation would not have been sterilized. We can only imagine how clean the 'operating room' would have been.

In 1834, James Simpson discovered how to use the gas chloroform as a general anaesthetic for surgical operations.

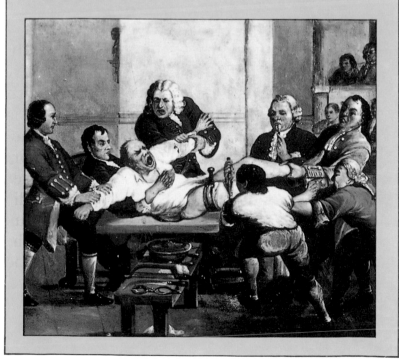

There were several theories to explain why sepsis occurred. Some people believed it was caused by the oxygen in the air, and so they tried to make wound dressings that would keep out the air – even by holding the wound under water. Others believed that the problem lay in the hospital buildings themselves; they said that all the old hospitals should be pulled down and replaced with new ones in order to cure what they called 'hospitalism'.

It is true that hospitals in those days were far from healthy places in which to be. Sick people were crowded together and, in addition to the 'normal' risks of having to undergo an operation, patients were likely to catch tuberculosis, a disease that spreads quickly in overcrowded

A scene in a women's ward at a London hospital in about 1810. The ward was probably nowhere near as clean and light at it appears in this picture.

Florence Nightingale at Scutari

The hospital for wounded soldiers was in an old army barracks at Scutari, in Turkey. It was poorly equipped, dirty, damp and filled with the stench of open sewers that flowed beneath it.

When she arrived from England with her team of thirty-eight nurses, Florence began to organize the hospital. She arranged for medical equipment to be bought, and set about cleaning up the wards and getting them painted. She also hired a house for use as a laundry where bedding could be washed. The clean, well-equipped hospitals that we have today owe much to the pioneering work of Florence Nightingale, both in the Crimean War and when she returned to Britain.

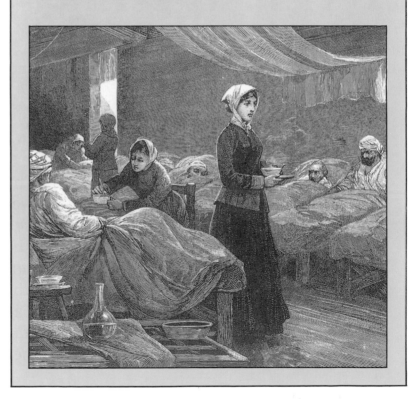

conditions and especially among people who are poorly nourished. Florence Nightingale was one of the first people of her time to realize this, when she nursed wounded soldiers during the Crimean War of 1853–56.

In 1848, as he was getting ready to begin studying at University College Hospital, Lister became ill with smallpox. Perhaps because he was anxious not to miss any classes, he began his studies too soon instead of waiting until he was fully recovered. As a result he became ill again. This time he was advised to rest until he was completely well. He spent several months convalescing in Ireland and then returned to London at the end of the year.

Lister's studies began with anatomy (the structure of the human body) and physiology

The Old Hospital at University College, London. Lister studied there to become a doctor from 1848 to 1850.

(how the body works). He was fortunate to have good teachers, in particular Professors Sharpey and Wharton Jones, to share their knowledge and stimulate his enquiring mind.

He was a hard-working student. Besides attending classes and working in the hospital wards, he also found time to carry out research of his own using a microscope. He became especially interested in the muscles that control the iris, or coloured part of the eye. A German surgeon, Professor Kölliker, had discovered that there were tiny muscles, called smooth muscles, in some parts of the body including the iris. Unlike the so-called striped muscles which we can work voluntarily to move our face, arms and legs,

An early photograph of Joseph Lister, at the age of twenty-eight.

14

smooth muscles act involuntarily, beyond our control. Kölliker reasoned that the smooth muscles in the iris contract and relax to change the size of the dark part of the eye, or pupil, to control the amount of light entering the eye.

Professor Wharton Jones, an eye surgeon himself, had arrived at the same conclusion, but he asked Lister to study the matter in more depth. By dissecting human and animal eyes, Lister discovered that there were two layers of muscle in the iris – one which reduces the size of the pupil in bright light and another which enlarges it in the dark.

Above Professor Rudolf von Kölliker, who discovered the so-called smooth muscles in the body. Lister found that there are two layers of smooth muscles in the human eye.

Opposite Medical students at a lecture in a university hospital in 1882.

Right Professor William Sharpey, one of Lister's teachers at University College Hospital, London.

Professor James Syme was a brilliant surgeon who worked in Edinburgh. In 1853 Lister went to visit him for a month; he remained in Scotland for the next twenty-four years.

Following on from his work on the eye, Lister looked at the muscles which make people's hair stand on end when they are cold or frightened. He then made the first detailed drawings of these tiny muscles. After carefully recording his observations and theories, he wrote scientific papers on these two areas of research and published them shortly after he qualified as a doctor.

Not surprisingly, Lister's efforts paid off. He gained very high marks in his degree of Bachelor of Medicine and Surgery and was awarded two university gold medals. Two years later, in 1852, after yet more study, he passed the examination to become a Fellow of the Royal College of Surgeons of England.

At that time young surgeons were encouraged to visit medical centres and hospitals in Europe to further their training and increase their knowledge. Professor Sharpey suggested, instead, that Lister should visit Edinburgh to spend a month with Professor James Syme, a brilliant surgeon. Lister took his advice and in 1853 he travelled to Scotland; he remained there for the next twenty-four years.

Lister is often thought of as being a Scot, probably because he spent so long in Scotland and carried out his most important work there. He went to Edinburgh in 1853 intending at first to stay only for a month, but shortly after his arrival he was offered the chance to become Professor Syme's house-surgeon and assistant. This was an opportunity to gain more experience in treating patients and teaching students, and Lister gladly accepted.

Another factor may well have encouraged him to stay – Agnes Syme, the Professor's daughter. They were attracted to each other and soon they

The surgical hospital of the Old Royal Infirmary in Edinburgh, were Lister and Professor Syme taught and worked.

In 1856 Lister married Agnes Syme, the daughter of Professor James Syme.

fell in love. As a member of the Society of Friends, Lister could not marry someone who was not a Quaker so he resigned from the Society. He joined Agnes in attending the Episcopalian Church. They were married in April 1856 and spent their honeymoon in Italy.

When they returned, Lister continued his work with James Syme. Agnes was deeply interested in her husband's studies and she helped him with his experiments and in writing up his notes. In 1855 Lister had become a Fellow of the Royal College of Surgeons of Scotland and the following year he was promoted to Assistant Surgeon and Lecturer in Surgery. By 1857 he was able to take charge of a ward when senior surgeons were absent, and was extremely capable of performing the operations that were carried out at that time.

Early Experiments

As a child, Lister had been fascinated by the study of animals and plants. During his early years as a surgeon in Edinburgh, he spent many nights experimenting on animals in order to discover how inflammation occurred after injury. He observed the frogs' webbed feet and bats' wings through his microscope and made detailed drawings of what he saw.

This drawing Lister made of the webbed foot of a frog shows how the blood vessels dilate, or expand, after heat has been applied. If the injury was not too great, the vessels returned to their normal size. If the heat was applied for a longer period they remained dilated, became blocked with red corpuscles and the blood clotted. The black spots are the pigmented (coloured) cells in the frog's skin.

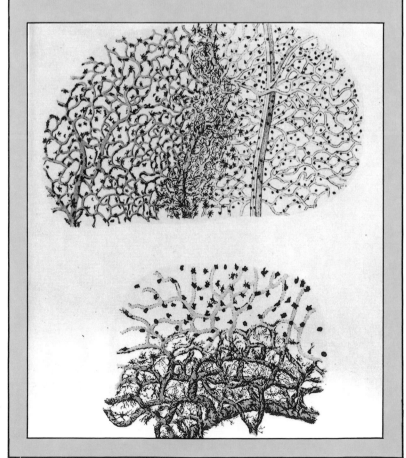

Coagulation of Blood

One of Lister's earliest experiments was to test the theory that blood outside the body coagulates (clots) because of the escape of ammonia.

He inserted a rubber tube into the jugular vein of a sheep so that the blood flowed through the tube. While the blood was circulating, the tube was tied into a number of airtight receptacles. Lister examined the blood in these receptacles at various intervals. He observed that the blood in the airtight receptacles coagulated as quickly as it would have done if in contact with air. Because ammonia could not have escaped from the receptacles, the experiment implied that ammonia does not affect the coagulation of blood.

(Below) Lister used this apparatus in an experiment to show why blood coagulates outside the body.

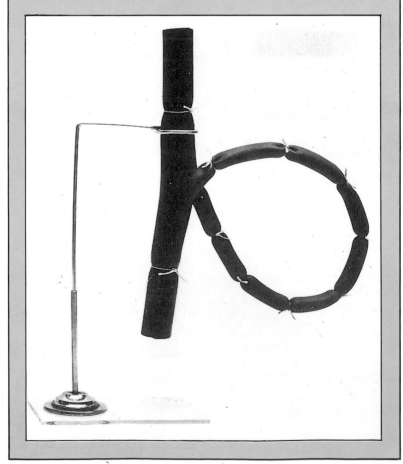

Lister used this apparatus in an experiment to show why blood clots, or coagulates, outside the body.

Despite his long hours of work in the operating theatre, wards and lecture room of Edinburgh's Old Royal Infirmary, Lister still found time to continue his research. Having studied the smooth muscles in the eye and skin, he began to observe how they worked in blood vessels. By examining animals through his microscope he saw how the blood's red corpuscles move through narrow blood vessels called capillaries. He saw that the capillaries were just large enough to allow the red corpuscles to pass through one at a time. When he put hot water on the web of a frog's foot he noticed that the capillaries enlarged, allowing corpuscles to pass three at a time, and then returned to normal. As he increased the heat of the water and the number of times he applied it, the capillaries ceased to return to their normal size and filled up with corpuscles, and the blood became sticky and clotted. Frogs are cold-blooded creatures and Lister now repeated his experiment with a warm-blooded animal – a bat – and got exactly the same results when he put hot water on its wing.

A bat in flight. Following Lister's experiments on frogs, which are cold-blooded creatures, he observed how blood clots form when the wing of a warm-blooded bat is damaged.

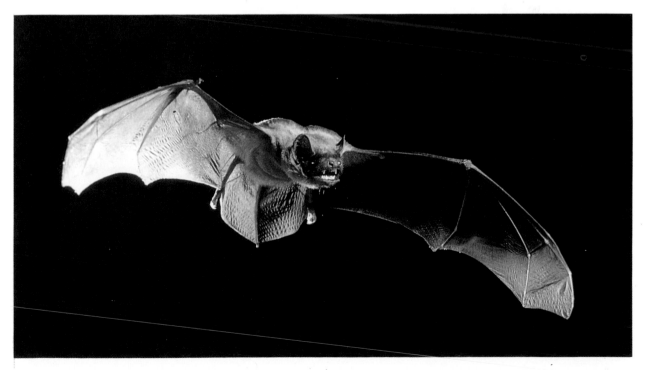

He was witnessing the start of what we call inflammation, which occurs when the body suffers a wound. You have probably noticed how your skin becomes red when it is scratched or sunburned. It may be that if Lister had continued his observations into the night, he would have seen the blood's white cells move through the walls of the capillaries and clear away the dead corpuscles. As it was, these actions of the white blood cells were not discovered until 1867 and 1883.

Lister published scientific papers describing his experiments, and in 1860 he was rewarded for his pioneering work by being elected a Fellow of the Royal Society. In the same year he was offered the post of Regius Professor of Surgery in Glasgow. He was still only thirty-seven years old and the appointment was a great honour.

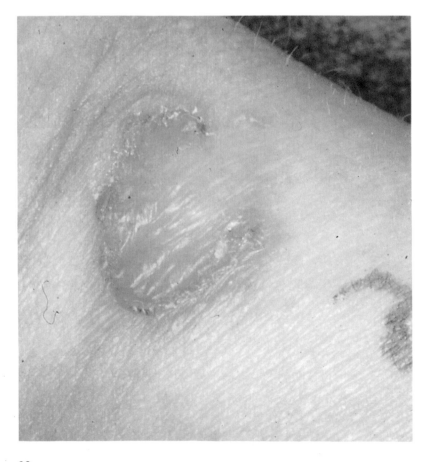

Inflammation of the skin. This inflamed sore was caused by an infection.

Lister at the age of forty-two. By this time he had moved from Edinburgh to work at the Royal Infirmary in Glasgow.

He spent his first year in Glasgow teaching students and did not carry out his first operation there until 1861. He was full of ideas on how surgical techniques might be improved, but at first he had difficulty even getting enough extra beds for his patients in the hospital. More importantly, there was the ever-present danger of sepsis ocurring after an operation; Lister knew that surgery could not be improved until a solution was found to this problem.

Lister was fully aware of the theories concerning why sepsis occurred (see Chapter 2) and he tried out for himself the wound dressings that it was thought might prevent it. Although he had no more success than other surgeons, he was convinced that the cause of sepsis was something to do with the air. After all, he reasoned, if the skin remains unbroken the body is protected and, what is more, he had noticed that when a scab forms over a wound it gives some protection to the flesh underneath.

He also tried to do something to reduce the causes of 'hospitalism'. He made sure his ward was always kept clean and he reduced the

Glasgow in the mid-nineteenth century. In 1860, Lister moved to Glasgow to become Regius Professor of Surgery. Most of his work on antisepsis was carried out at the Royal Infirmary there.

overcrowding. But little more than a metre from the wall of his ward he found a mass of buried coffins – the result of a cholera epidemic that occurred in 1849 – and nearby was a barely covered burial pit. Clearly, Lister's efforts to clean up the ward were only a small step towards preventing the spread of infection.

It was at this time that he first heard of the work being done by a French chemist, Louis Pasteur. A colleague in Glasgow, Dr Thomas Anderson, drew Lister's attention to an article Pasteur had written in a chemistry journal. It described how Pasteur had found proof that the air contains tiny living things – microbes or germs – that cause wine to ferment and then to decay. He was saying, in effect, that the decay does not happen spontaneously and that it is not caused by oxygen or the air itself. Lister knew immediately that Pasteur could well be right; he also realized that the Frenchman's experiments were quite simple to perform and test.

A surgical operation in progress in about 1870. Compare the operating room and the clothes of the doctors and nurses with those in the picture of a modern operation on page 45.

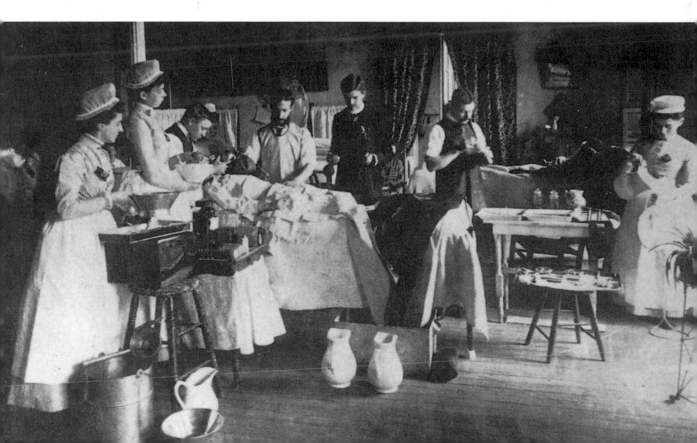

Louis Pasteur in his laboratory

Louis Pasteur carried out experiments on wine in France, to try to discover why it went bad when left exposed to the air. He boiled a liquid containing yeast to kill off any organisms it contained, and then left it to cool. Air was allowed to come into contact with the liquid, but in some of his samples dust and microbes were kept out while in other samples they too could reach the yeast. The samples exposed to air and microbes became contaminated, while those exposed only to air remained free of organisms. In this way Pasteur showed that it was not air itself that caused wine to go bad, but the microbes that float in air.

Within a very short time he carried out Pasteur's experiments and achieved exactly the same results. Although many other scientists failed to understand the relevance of Pasteur's findings,

Lister devised a method of moving liquid from one flask to another without it becoming contaminated by bacteria.

Lister quickly grasped the idea that if invisible germs in the air could cause wine to decay, they might also be responsible for the sepsis that so often affected wounds. Pasteur had found that the germs could be killed by heat. Lister knew that this method could not be used on wounds; perhaps there was another way. Again, Dr Anderson was able to help.

Thirty years earlier a chemical called carbolic acid had been discovered. It was used, in the form of creosote, to prevent the wood of railway sleepers from rotting, and to control the decay of sewage. Lister thought that if it could reduce decay in these materials it might also prevent or cure sepsis in wounds. Anderson was able to give him some creosote which contained carbolic acid.

Lister was determined to test his theory by using carbolic acid on a patient, but he knew it had to be on someone with injuries so severe that he or she could not normally be expected to survive.

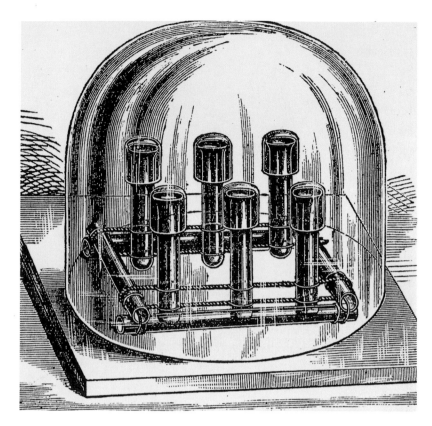

This apparatus was developed by Lister for cultivating micro-organisms.

In March 1865 he found a man with just such injuries. He put carbolic acid in the man's dressings but unfortunately this seemed to have little effect and the patient died. Although this upset him greatly, Lister still believed his theory was correct.

His next patient was an eleven-year-old boy who had been run over by a cart. Both his legs were broken and so was the skin. Lister instructed his house-surgeon to dip a dressing into carbolic acid and cover the wound with it. Both broken legs were then set and put into splints to support them while they mended. For the next four days everything went well, but then the boy's wound became painful. Removing the dressing, Lister saw that a scab had formed and the wound was healing. He realized that the pain was caused by the carbolic acid burning the skin. When the dressing was changed the pain eased and the boy recovered fully.

Not satisfied with just one good result on a patient whom, he told himself, might have survived anyway, Lister continued his experiments. By the beginning of 1867 he had treated thirteen more people who had serious bone fractures. The first patient had died and the third, although doing well at the start, had developed gangrene while Lister was away from Glasgow. He decided that in future he would do all the dressings himself. Some of the later patients might, he thought, have survived even without the carbolic acid dressings, but there were seven others whose injuries tested his ideas to the limit. These seven had injuries which, in normal circumstances, would have meant that it would have been necessary to amputate an arm or leg. Thanks to Lister's treatment and skill all seven survived without the need for amputation.

At last he was convinced he had the evidence he needed and he wrote a scientific paper describing all thirteen cases and others in which less serious infections had been cured. His paper was published in the medical journal *The Lancet*, in March and April 1867.

Lister's surgical instruments.

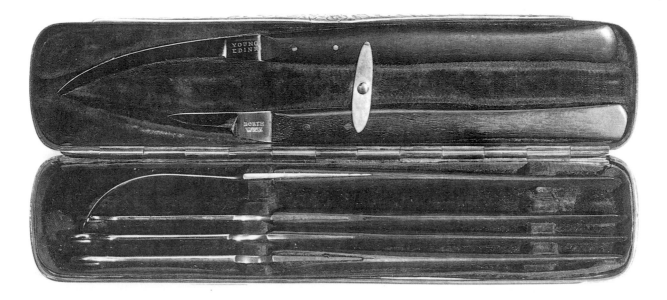

Now that he was satisfied that carbolic acid really did work, Lister began to improve the dressings. Because the creosote burned the patients' skin, he tried using crystals of pure carbolic acid. This could also cause burns and it had to be diluted to make it weaker. However, the crystals did not dissolve very well in water so he tried various types of oil instead. After experimenting with linseed oil he eventually decided on paraffin oil.

He believed that if a dressing were to be truly effective it should resemble as closely as possible nature's own protection against germs – a scab. This meant it must be flexible so that it could be moulded to the shape of the injured part of the body. To achieve this he dissolved carbolic acid in paraffin oil and mixed it with a putty-like resin.

Lister then looked for the best fabric to use in making the dressings. He decided upon a type of cotton material called muslin. Knowing that a scab

In November 1868, Lister wrote to his father about his attempt to prevent the stump of an amputated leg from becoming contaminated by micro-organisms. This diagram, which was part of his letter, shows the stump (L) covered with a rubber tube (I). Pieces of cloth soaked in carbolic acid (CA1 and CA2) were used to destroy the micro-organisms that would cause sepsis.

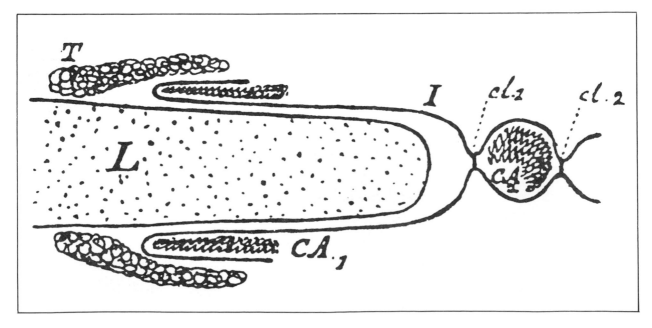

does not let in any air or fluid, he then tried placing a piece of thin metal foil between layers of oiled silk. Later he found that thin mackintosh, which was used for making the lining in hats, was even better. He discovered that his new dressings had to be kept in boxes to keep them damp and stop the carbolic acid from evaporating. When he used a dressing, he first placed some layers of muslin, soaked in carbolic acid, next to the skin and then applied the dressing itself.

Other surgeons had caught on to Lister's ideas and were trying other chemicals besides carbolic acid, such as salicylic acid and boracic acid. Lister also continued to experiment with new substances, including chemicals made from mercury and zinc. One of these proved ideal because it killed germs, did not irritate the skin and could be used with carbolic acid. As more and more surgeons wanted to use these new dressings, companies were formed to manufacture them. In Britain, T.J. Smith started what is now Smith and Nephew, a company that makes many medical products, while in the United States, R.W. Johnson set up Johnson and Johnson.

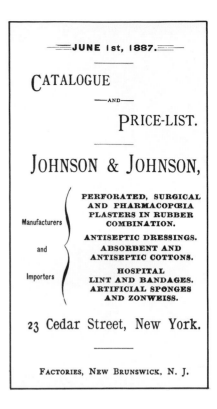

Above *A catalogue of the pharmaceutical company Johnson & Johnson from 1887. Among the goods advertised were antiseptic dressings.*

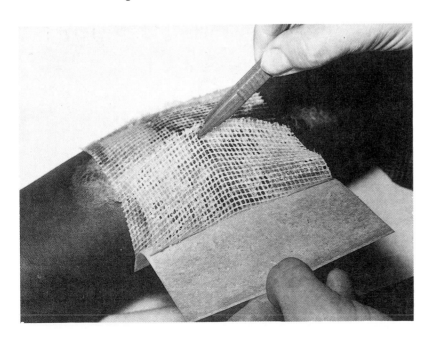

Left *A modern antiseptic gauze dressing is applied to a wound.*

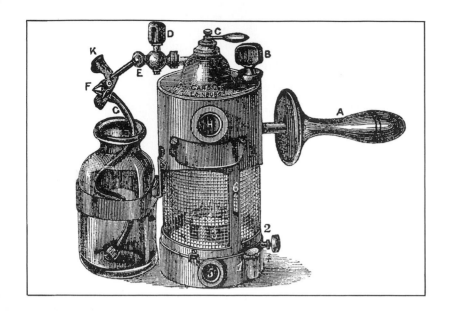

This spray, invented by Lister, was designed to fill an operating room with steam and carbolic acid vapour.

Lister's next development was rather less successful than his dressings. He thought that a device which produced a fine spray of carbolic acid around the patient during an operation might help to keep the wound germ-free. He invented a number of different machines to do this, ranging from small hand-held pumps to larger steam-powered devices. However, it was found that carbolic acid could actually damage sensitive parts inside the body and that germs could be spread by water or by dirt on people's hands or on the machines. As a result the spray was abandoned.

He next turned his attention to the materials used during operations. When a surgeon cuts a patient open, he or she has to cut through arteries and veins. To prevent too much blood being lost, the cut ends of the blood vessels are pinched together and tied with pieces of silk or linen thread, called ligatures. When the ties are used to stitch together parts of the body, such as intestines or skin, they are known as sutures. In Lister's time the ligature was tied around the blood vessel and one end was left hanging from the wound to be removed later when the wound suppurated, or produced pus.

Incredible as it seems to us now, in Lister's day these same blood-stained ligatures would then be used again and again. Young doctors and medical students would carry the ligatures around in the buttonholes of their coats and hand them to the surgeon when they were required during an operation. The more blood-stained the ligatures were, the more daring the surgeon was thought to be.

During this operation, performed in Edinburgh in about 1870, a carbolic acid spray is being used.

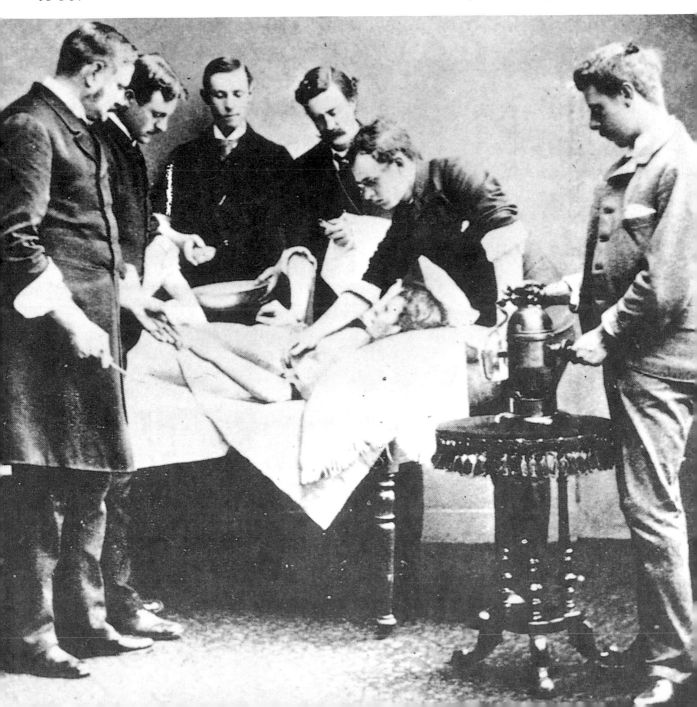

Realizing that the re-used ligatures must spread infection from one patient to the next, Lister began experimenting by soaking a ligature in a solution of carbolic acid. In December 1867 he operated on an old horse. After cutting an artery he tied the ligature, cut the ends short and put on an antiseptic dressing. The wound healed well. Six weeks later, when the horse died of old age, Lister looked at the ligature; it was still tied in place and there had been no suppuration.

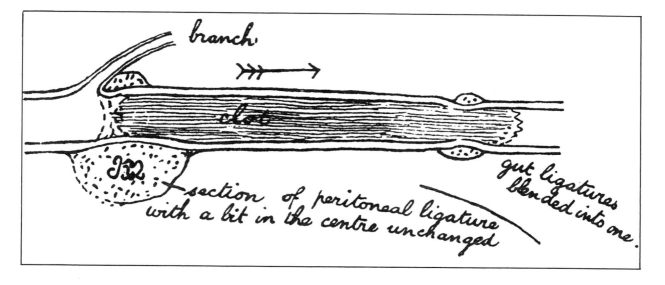

This drawing by Lister shows the result of a successful operation carried out using catgut ligatures soaked in carbolic acid.

He then tried his new technique on a human patient. A woman came to him with an aneurysm of the thigh – a bulging artery caused by a weakness of its wall. It was important to operate on the aneurysm because the patient could bleed to death if the artery burst. As before, Lister operated, tied the sterilized ligature and cut the ends short. The wound healed very quickly. After several months, however, she died suddenly following the bursting of another aneurysm. Lister was able to examine the ligature and found that it had remained secure.

Even though he realized that at last he could perform operations with much more safety, Lister was not content to let things stand still. He tried

34

sterilizing ligatures made from another material, catgut, which was made from the intestines of sheep and used for violin strings. He operated on a calf using catgut ligatures and was completely successful. What is more, he found that the catgut seemed to blend with the body and almost disappeared after a few weeks.

It was vital to sterilize the catgut completely to kill the germs, including tetanus, which occur in sheep's intestines. The sterilization process was slow, however, and some surgeons who did not perform the process thoroughly found that tetanus developed. Lister looked for other, faster methods of sterilization, and finally decided to use the chemicals mercury perchloride and chromium sulphate.

Lister's next task was to find a way of joining broken bones while they mended. He successfully used silver wire to mend a broken kneecap and later developed pegs of sterilized ivory and steel to join together longer broken bones. Similar steel pegs, as well as plates and screws, are used extensively in modern surgery.

Yet another of Lister's innovations involved using rubber tubes to drain pus from abscesses in the body. The first of his patients to benefit from

A modern artificial hip joint, showing the metal ball and pin, which is inserted into the bone of the leg, and the plastic hip socket. Lister was the first surgeon to develop sterilized ivory and steel pegs with which to join broken bones.

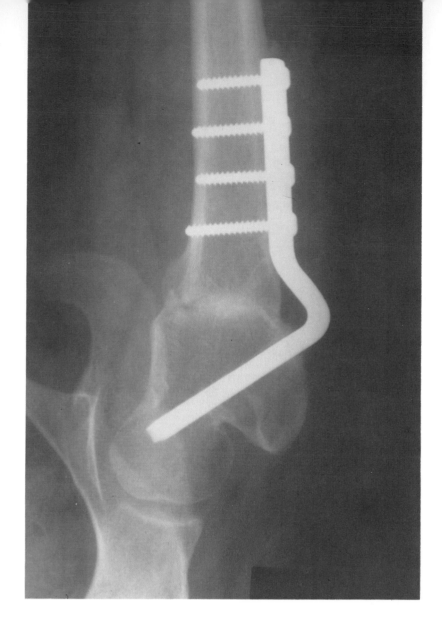

this was Queen Victoria, who in 1871 had a painful abscess in her armpit. Lister tried draining the pus through a piece of lint he had inserted, but with little success. It occurred to him that the abscess would continue to drain if a piece of rubber tubing were inserted in place of the lint. At the same time he was using a carbolic spray, much to the displeasure of the Queen, who complained that the carbolic acid stung her eyes. Lister cut a piece of tubing and soaked it overnight in carbolic acid. The following day he inserted it and the abscess cleared up quickly.

In spite of all his successes, Lister was not immediately acclaimed. Some surgeons tried his methods but did not follow his directions properly, and lost interest when things did not turn out as they had expected. Others refused to believe that microbes in the air even existed. A few were simply jealous of his achievements in surgery. In all it was twelve years from the time he published his article in *The Lancet* in 1867 until his breakthrough was finally acknowledged.

During that time Lister moved first back to Edinburgh and then, in 1877, to London. He would probably not have returned to London at all had it not been for the fact that the surgeons there were highly suspicious of his work. He knew he had to convince them.

A demonstration of surgery at Charing Cross Hospital, London, in 1900. Lister's antiseptic techniques were well-accepted by that time.

Although he had experienced opposition from many of his medical colleagues in Britain (though not from those in Edinburgh and Glasgow), surgeons in Denmark and Germany were achieving dramatic results with Lister's methods. One of these surgeons, Professor Nussbaum of Germany, had seen 80 per cent of his patients die of hospital gangrene in 1874; by 1876, after using Lister's techniques for just over a year, this infection barely occurred at all.

While surgeons in other countries and in other parts of Britain were gradually being won over, many of those in London had not even troubled to find out about antisepsis. Fortunately a few were convinced, and they persuaded the Governors of King's College Hospital, London, to allow Lister to become an extra Professor of Surgery and to bring with him a team of doctors and nurses from Edinburgh.

King's College Hospital, London, where Lister became a Professor of Surgery in 1877.

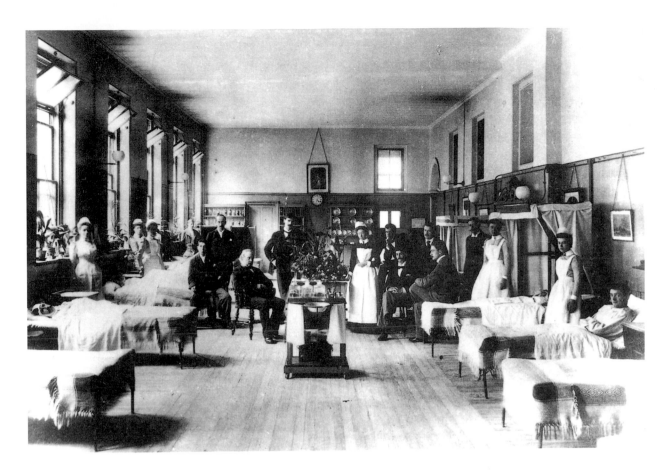

It was still an uphill struggle, however. At first Lister and his team were given few beds in the hospital and no patients, and the students they taught were only interested in cramming in knowledge about the accepted methods of surgery in order to pass their exams. Yet, within two years of arriving back in London, Lister had achieved his aim. The lectures he gave, in which he demonstrated Pasteur's experiment and his own developments, stimulated surgeons to send him difficult cases that no one else dared operate on. Sometimes, no doubt, they were hoping that he would fail, but when his operations proved startlingly successful they changed their views. More and more surgeons now came to learn his techniques and, by putting them into practice, they were able to devise new operations to cure disease.

Lister with his staff in the Victoria ward at King's College Hospital in 1893, shortly before his retirement.

Lister addressing the British Association, of which he was President, in 1896. His speech was about the way in which medicine and the other branches of science are all related.

In 1879 Lister travelled to Amsterdam, in the Netherlands, to address five hundred surgeons and doctors from all over Europe at the International Congress of Medical Science. When he had finished speaking, the entire audience rose to its feet, cheering and clapping. Following that, he was awarded countless honours, medals, degrees and diplomas by scientific and medical societies, universities and cities throughout Europe. In 1883 he was knighted by Queen Victoria and became Sir Joseph Lister. Fourteen years later he became the first doctor to be made a Peer of the House of Lords. After Victoria's death (in 1901), Edward VII came to the throne and included Lister in the first group of distinguished men to receive the Order of Merit. Meanwhile, in 1895, he had been elected President of the Royal Society.

Lister (in the centre) and Louis Pasteur (second from the left) at the Sorbonne in Paris, 1892. The occasion was Pasteur's seventieth birthday.

Among the greatest pleasures in Lister's life were his meetings with Louis Pasteur. Although their work had linked them ever since 1865, they did not meet until 1881 when Pasteur came to London. The two men admired each other's work enormously and became firm friends.

Lister was knighted in 1883 and became a Peer of the House of Lords in 1897.

Eventually, at the age of sixty-six, Lister retired. In 1903, towards the end of his life, his eyesight began to fail. Five years later he moved from London to Walmer, in Kent. In 1912 he caught pneumonia and died on 10 February. After a service in Westminster Abbey he was buried, as he had requested, next to his wife in Hampstead cemetery in London.

Joseph Lister has been called the 'Father of Modern Surgery'. Even a brief study of his work shows that this is a very fitting title. Without his antiseptic methods, surgery could not have developed from the way it was in the 1840s, when countless patients died following operations that would otherwise have saved them.

But Lister did not simply make the operations that were carried out in his time more successful; his antisepsis actually made it possible to perform completely new types of surgery that had previously been impossible. This is still true today.

Lister was the first person to realize how wounds become infected. People in all branches of medicine now know that it is essential to stop harmful bacteria from coming into contact with wounds. This nurse is sterilizing dental instruments.

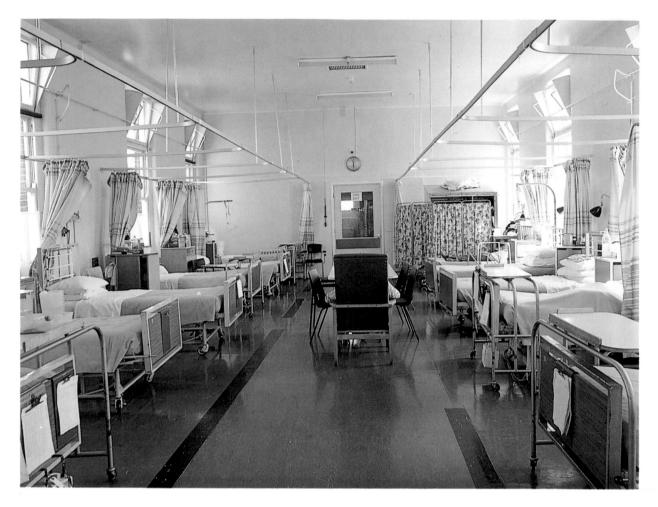

The remarkable improvements in surgery which have led to the transplantation of organs – such as kidneys, livers and even hearts – could never have been put into practice unless surgeons knew that the operation wounds could be protected from germs. The same applies to the removal of an appendix or a cancerous tumour.

Lister's work is a good example of how discoveries in one field can lead to advances in another. It was the discovery by Pasteur – a chemist – of microbes in the air that led Lister – a surgeon – to find and cure the cause of sepsis.

Unlike many of his contemporaries, Lister was always prepared to listen to the ideas of others, both in his own scientific field and in others. For example, he was pleased when some surgeons

A light, clean ward in a modern hospital. Before Lister's time, infections and diseases often spread through wards from patient to patient.

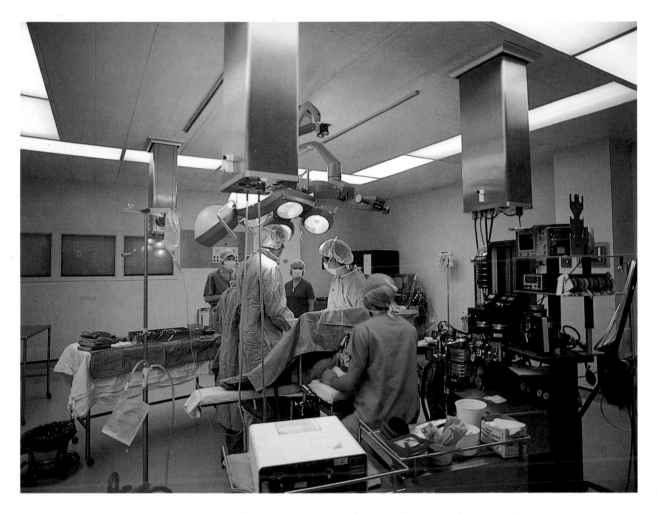

An operating theatre in a modern hospital in the United States.

began experimenting with other antiseptic chemicals besides carbolic acid; as long as these chemicals killed germs and prevented infection he recognized them as being useful. He was also, undoubtedly, a fine surgeon.

Yet, in addition to these two valuable characteristics, Lister possessed another which was, perhaps, even more important; perseverence. When, in 1865, the first patient he treated using antiseptic dressings died, Lister did not give up the struggle. He was sure that his ideas were right and his next operation helped to prove it. What is more, even when he knew he had succeeded in defeating sepsis he did not rest but continually tried to improve his techniques and the materials he used.

Date Chart

1827 Joseph Lister born at Upton House, outside London, on 5 April.

1835–44 Attended Quaker schools in Hertfordshire and North London.

1844–47 Studied for matriculation and Bachelor of Arts degree at University College, London.

1848 Caught smallpox. Became a medical student at University College Hospital.

1850 Qualified as a doctor.

1852 Became a Fellow of the Royal College of Surgeons of England.

1853 Scientific papers on the eye and skin published. Travelled to Edinburgh.

1856 Married Agnes Syme.

1860 Appointed Regius Professor of Surgery at Glasgow.

1865 Learned of experiments done by Louis Pasteur. Began using carbolic acid in wound dressings.

1867 Article on antiseptic dressings published in *The Lancet*. Developed sterilized ligatures and other surgical materials.

1869 Developed carbolic acid spray (abandoned in 1887).

1871 Operated on Queen Victoria.

1877 Returned to London to work at King's College Hospital.

1879 His antiseptic principle finally accepted.

1883 Baronetcy conferred by Queen Victoria – became Sir Joseph Lister.

1893 Retired. Agnes died.

1895 Elected President of the Royal Society.

1903 Eyesight began to fail.

1908 Moved to Walmer, Kent.

1912 Died at Walmer, 10 February. Buried in Hampstead.

Glossary

Abscess A collection of pus in the body.

Achromatic lens A lens through which light can pass without being split into the colours of the rainbow.

Anaesthetics Drugs that produce unconsciousness or numbness for a period of time.

Antisepsis The destruction of harmful organisms – literally 'against sepsis'.

Antiseptic A substance that destroys harmful bacteria.

Arteries Blood vessels that carry blood from the heart to other parts of the body.

Bacteria Tiny living organisms found in the soil, the air, dust and on the body. They are also called germs or microbes.

Capillaries Tiny blood vessels that carry blood to the cells of the body. Blood enters the capillaries from arteries and leaves through veins to return to the heart.

Carbolic acid A substance found in coal tar. It is also known as phenol.

Cholera A severe illness that affects the intestines. It can now be prevented and is rare in developed countries, but it still affects thousands of people in the developing world.

Cold-blooded A name for creatures whose body temperature varies according to the temperature of their surroundings.

Convalesce To recover from an illness, injury or operation.

Corpuscles Red blood corpuscles carry oxygen to the cells of the body. White corpuscles can surround bacteria and carry away dead cells.

Dissect To cut open an animal or plant and inspect it closely.

Dressing A covering for a wound.

Gangrene The death and decay of bodily tissue caused by disease, injury or an interruption of the blood supply.

Infection Invasion of the body by bacteria, viruses and fungi.

Inflammation The reaction which occurs when a part of the body is injured or infected. It is usually indicated by redness, pain and swelling.

Ligature A piece of material, such as silk, thread, catgut or fine wire, used to tie a blood vessel during an operation.

Mackintosh Waterproof, rubberized material.

Microbes Another name for bacteria.

Pus The fluid produced by an inflammation, consisting of live and dead bacteria, dead white corpuscles and other dead cells.

Scab The tough crust that forms over a wound.

Sepsis The decay and poisoning that comes from an infection caused by bacteria.

Smallpox A dangerous, highly contagious disease.

Sterilize To make something free from bacteria.

Suture The thread used for stitching up parts of the body in an operation.

Tetanus An acute, infectious disease caused by bacteria present in soil.

Warm-blooded A name for animals whose body temperature remains constant, usually above the temperature of their surroundings.

Books to Read

Health and Medicine by Brenda Walpole (Wayland, 1990)

The Body in Question by Jonathan Miller (Cape, 1978)

The Human Body Atlas by Mark Crocker (Oxford University Press, 1991)

Medical Technology by Mark Lambert (Wayland, 1990)

Picture acknowledgements

The publishers would like to thank the following for the use of the photographs in this book; Bruce Coleman 21 (Frank Greenaway); Mary Evans 4, 11, 24, 26, 37, 38; Hulton Picture Company 23, 40, 41; Mansell Collection iii, 25, 33, 42; Ann Ronan Picture Library 8, 10, 14, 15, 28, 30, 32, 34; Science Photo Library 22, 35, 36, 44, 45; Wayland Picture Library cover, 5, 6, 9, 12, 13, 16, 17, 18, 19, 20, 27, 29, 31 (both), 39, 43. Cover artwork is by Richard Hook.

Index